ENCHANTING NEW MEXICO

BY SUSAN HAZEN-HAMMOND

DESIGNED BY RICHARD C. SANDOVAL

ENCHANTING NEW MEXICO is a colorful book that starts where *New Mexico Magazine* leaves off—capturing the enchantment of the state you love with over one hundred beautiful pictures. One hundred color filled pages guide you on a personal tour of New Mexico, a tour to enjoy and share with friends.

New Mexico magazine
Publications Group

4

First paperback edition 1984
by New Mexico Magazine

Published by New Mexico Magazine

ISBN: 0-937206-04-0

New Mexico Magazine
Bataan Memorial Building
Santa Fe, New Mexico 87503

Library of Congress Catalog
Card Number 84-062288

*The sun sets on a ranch in the Tularosa
Basin (cover), west of the San Andrés
Mountains in southern New Mexico
(photo by Mark Nohl), and rises in
the Guadalupe Mountains (first
page, photo by Jim Bones). Overleaf,
a New Mexico autumn scene, when
summer's green aspens and
cottonwoods turn gold (photo by
Mark Nohl).*

Gail Haggard

The graceful head of the Rocky Mountain Bee Plant. In mountainous areas and at low elevations after a rain, hundreds of wildflowers blossom. Desert cactus typically blooms in March and April; mountain wildflowers are often most profuse in August and September.

CONTENTS

6

The pasqueflower, or "windflower," one of dozens of species of colorful wildflowers that attract photographers and nature lovers to New Mexico.

FOREWORD

Five short years ago I sat in my small dining room overlooking the Strait of Juan de Fuca, which separates Washington State's lush Olympic Peninsula from Vancouver Island, British Columbia, and tried to decide where to spend an upcoming year's leave of absence from my job and everyday life. Europe, my first choice, was out of the question. So at the little table looking out on the cold waters of the northern Pacific, I studied state maps and travel guides, without having any clear sense of a good second choice.

Then suddenly one day I knew: I would spend my year in New Mexico. It didn't matter that until then I'd just seen the place in passing through on the way to other destinations. It would be an adventure, I was sure.

Five years later my one-year leave of absence has transmuted itself into a more-or-less permanent move and a new way of life. New Mexico has provided all the adventure I expected—and more. Sometimes as I sit in my simple backyard patio in Santa Fe overlooking a sea of white desert primroses, pink and burgundy hollyhocks, and wild sunflowers, I still fantasize about gypsying off to Europe for a year, but not very seriously. Santa Fe in particular and New Mexico in general hold much the same attraction that Europe does, to me: a complicated blend of languages, history, cultures, and people that provides an endless fountain of experiences, insights, ideas, dramas, and dreams. Each village and town seems to glow with its own charm (sometimes through a layer of dust), whether the population is primarily Hispanics, Indians, Johnny-come-lately Anglos, or—as often occurs—some novel mixture of all three.

The editors and publishers of **New Mexico Magazine** have long been aware of this magical combination of ingredients, and for over sixty years they have provided readers a kaleidoscope of glimpses into the land and its people. This book is partly an outgrowth of that editorial ambition: to reveal to readers what it is about New Mexico that makes it a special place.

The photographs presented here come from the pages of **New Mexico Magazine**, byproducts of the sensitive perceptions of photographers seeking to capture the moods of the state. The text is all new. It is dedicated to my family and to my partner, Eduardo Fuss. As I was researching and writing, he cooked, cleaned, ran errands, held my hand, encouraged me, helped me laugh, and pointed me in the direction of the dinner table. Special thanks, too, to the staff at the New Mexico State Library and to Richard Sandoval, editor of the book publishing division of **New Mexico Magazine**, who conceived the idea for this book.

Mark Nohl

High over the Tularosa Basin, summer thunderclouds begin to form. The summer rainy season brings frequent afternoon thunderstorms, spectacular lightning displays, and relatively cooler air. Site of ancient Indian petroglyphs in the Three Rivers Petroglyph area, the Tularosa Basin is also home to old lava flows, hardened centuries ago into striated, contorted formations among which visitors wander today at the Valley of Fires State Park near Carrizozo.

ENCHANTING LAND

New Mexico "extends a great way towards the North Pole," asserted the anonymous authors of **The Modern Part of an Universal History,** published in London in MDCCLXIII (1763). They admitted, however, that "the boundaries of this province are by no means ascertained."

Even so, "this will some day become the finest country in North America," they maintained confidently. Summer and winter here are "clear, healthy, and bracing," and the weather "is just what is desireable in season." Moreover, the people who live here are generous and peaceful—and small wonder, since they exist "in a state of more comfortable barbarity" than anywhere else in America. All in all, the writers concluded, "We may safely affirm that New Mexico is among the pleasantest, richest, and most plentiful countries in America, or any other part of the world."

Two centuries later, New Mexicans will tell you those anonymous prophet/historians were largely right—aside from that part about the North Pole (and you may even get some arguments there). Just as they predicted, New Mexico has become—or always has been, "the finest country in North America." Absolutely. Without a doubt.

After all, it's a land of skies so blue, waterfalls so sparkling, meadows so green, mountains so dramatic, villages so picturesque, and white desert sands so pure and mysterious that . . . well, frankly, that those describing these delights somehow tend to end up babbling.

Unfortunately, that just distorts the picture of what New Mexico really is. And for those seeking to know New Mexico, there's another problem, too. The natural beauties of the state notwithstanding, New Mexico often exists even more vividly in people's heads and hearts than it does out there on the other side of the car window or the camera lens.

That's where the terms "enchantment" and "enchanting land" come in. Way back in linguistic history, "enchantment" was part of the word we now know as "incantation." To enchant was to alter the perceptions of the listener in a spiritual or magical rite of chanting an incantation.

And that's what New Mexico seems to do. Given half a chance, the place may seem to sing you a chant that will alter your perceptions of yourself and the world, that will give you a special view of your own New Mexico. And the incantation you hear will differ slightly from the songs your neighbors hear, just as your New Mexico will differ at least slightly from theirs.

To the statistician, the tale lies in the numbers and the facts. In its 122,000 square miles, broken down into 33 counties, live 1.4 million people, most of Hispanic (37 percent), Indian (8 percent), and Anglo (53 percent) heritage. Its six vegetation zones range from that of the Lower Sonoran Desert, below about 4,200 feet elevation, to an Arctic-Alpine zone, above 12,000 feet high (justification, perhaps, for arguments that New Mexico does indeed reach "a great way towards the North Pole"). Its animal life includes over 400 species of birds. And on paper, at least, it might just as well be one big park, including, as it does, forty-four state parks, five state monuments, eleven national monuments and parks, and seven national recreation sites.

To the historian, by contrast, New Mexico sings of the past, of *conquistadores* like Francisco Vásquez de Coronado and Antonio de Espejo. Of the tragic "lost" colony of Gaspar Castaño de Sosa in 1591 and the first permanent Spanish settlement here in 1598, established by Don Juan de Oñate. Of the celebrated Pueblo Revolt of 1680 and the return of the Spanish a dozen years later. Of the Inquisition, whose influence extended even here. Of ancient inhabitants whose presence, in Clovis Man, dates back about 14,000 years. Of covered wagons, trapper's trails, Kit Carson, and Carson's brother-in-law Governor Bent, who was assassinated here on a cold January day in 1847.

To the archaeologist, the magic comes from the more than 25,000 prehistoric village sites in ruins around the state. To the anthropologist, it comes from languages forgotten and almost forgotten, from cultural diversity and colorful folkways found in such concentration in few other parts of the United States.

To the poet, to the artist, to the seeker of peace, New Mexico sings a song reflected today in volumes on bookstore and library shelves and in the paintings and drawings on art gallery walls across the nation.

And these are all outgrowths of the dozens and dozens of different ways of seeing this place and its present, future, and past. It's safe enough to affirm, 200 years later, 500 years later, 14,000 years later, that New Mexico is indeed still among the "pleasantest, richest, and most plentiful countries in America, or any part of the world." Just remember, though, that your New Mexico will be different from mine, and different from our neighbor's. Metaphorically speaking, the boundaries and limits of this "province" are still by no means ascertained.

A field of yucca plants near Carrizozo (right). Velas de Dios, *the early Spanish settlers called these abundant desert plants: the Candles of the Lord. The versatile yucca, which once supplied New Mexico's Indians with soap, food, and weaving fibers, is the state flower today. Below, a herd of Navajo sheep and goats clusters on a hilltop in the panoramic, arid wilderness of eastern Navajoland in the northwest corner of New Mexico. Throughout Navajo country native shepherds young and old spend their days tending flocks. Once restless nomads, the Navajos of today are known for their fine weavings, sand paintings, and jewelry, as well as their colorful clothing and quiet ways.*

Mark Nohl

Paul Logsdon

Mark Nohl

In the Angel Peak area of northwestern New Mexico, close to Farmington. Nearby, the Bisti Badlands and Chaco Culture National Historical Park lure sightseers down bumpy back roads through stark, dramatic countryside. Home to Anasazi Indians 1,000 years ago (Anasazi is a Navajo word meaning "ancient strangers"), the area is sparsely settled by hogan-dwelling Navajos today.

Mike Schneps

Russell Bamert

Mark Nohl

A golden autumn scene (above, left). Left, mule deer cross a rocky arroyo in the Guadalupe Mountains of southern New Mexico. Called "The Outside of Carlsbad Caverns" because of its proximity to the famous caves, the Guadalupe Range was once an ancient ocean reef.

The Organ Mountains in Doña Ana County, near Las Cruces. Don Juan de Oñate, who established the first Spanish colony in New Mexico in 1598, called these mountains "La Sierra del Olvido," the Mountains of Oblivion. In the late 1600s their name was changed to Los Organos, the Organ Mountains, because their ragged peaks resemble organ pipes. Old West days saw a rowdy mixture of miners and bandidos pass through here, and famed western sheriff Pat Garrett was shot to death in the foothills in 1908. Now instead of treasure seekers and desperadoes, the sheer, brittle rock faces of the "pipes" attract expert rock climbers and hikers.

Above, a waterfall splashes among the ferns in Lower Dog Canyon, leading out of the Sacramento Mountains in Oliver Lee Memorial State Park near Alamogordo. Pottery fragments, spear points, and thousands of other artifacts indicate the canyon has been occupied for at least 5,000 years. At right, Carlsbad Caverns National Park, southwest of Carlsbad. Besides a seemingly endless labyrinth of subterranean rooms and spectacular limestone formations, the caverns contain animal fossils dating back about 25,000 years. The park's famous bats winter in Mexico but spend their summers—from late May until October—in the caverns.

Jim Bones

Fallen leaves collect in the Pecos River near Terrero (above), and a quiet pool in the Pecos near Catfish Falls reflects the light (opposite). Beginning as a stream in Mora County in the eastern slopes of the Sangre de Cristo Mountains, the Pecos travels nearly 1,000 miles—over half of that in New Mexico—before joining the Río Grande. A pilgrimage along the Pecos leads through quiet Hispanic villages filled with ancient adobe houses, stone ruins, and old churches. Past Santa Rosa, "The City of Natural Lakes," and Billy the Kid's grave. Past the Bitter Lake National Wildlife Refuge and Carlsbad's in-triguing Living Desert State Park.

A GREAT TREASURE

Plese show me your greatest treasure," the conquistador asked his Indian host, who was heaping the Spaniards with gifts of food and cotton blankets. The explorers hoped to find gold.

The Indian motioned for the conquistador and his men to follow. On the banks of the Río Grande they stopped. "This is the most precious thing in life," the Indian said through an interpreter. He gestured towards the waters of the Río Grande, glistening gold in the pre-sunset light.

It's probably just a legend, historians say, but this story well illustrates how much we appreciate water in New Mexico. We love our sunshine, but clouds, too, are a blessing from nature. Every drop of rain is a gift, not to be squandered. Every lake and pond, every river and stream, is a great treasure.

When the Spaniards arrived, the Indians of New Mexico had already developed an efficient method of irrigation for bringing this fluid gold to their crops. Soon the Spanish built their own elaborate system of *acequias,* or irrigation canals, some of which survive today, still carrying water to apple orchards and chile fields. And for centuries nature has irrigated this dry land with rivers and streams and the erratic rush of flash floods in arroyos and empty stream beds.

Here rivers often flow just part time, depending on how much rain has fallen and how many users lay claim to the liquid treasure. Today, besides the Río Grande, our major waterways include the Pecos, the Chama, the San Juan, the Gila, and the Canadian, all luring enthusiastic recreationers and nature lovers. Added to the modest list of natural lakes—like the alpine lakes of the high mountains and the "bottomless" lakes and salt lakes of the plains— we've created a host of manmade lakes, such as mammoth Elephant Butte Lake in Sierra County and Navajo Lake in the northwestern corner of the state.

Many of these lie in state parks. In fact, most of our forty-four state parks, which encompass 165,000 scenic acres, include a lake, a river, or a stream. Like Bluewater Lake State Park, northwest of Grants in the Zuni Mountains at an elevation of 7,400 feet. As with many of our manmade lakes, Bluewater Lake began as an irrigation aid. In this case, in historical times, it was a French settler who in 1850 first altered the flow of Bluewater Creek to irrigate his farm. Soon more Frenchmen arrived and built a small earthen dam, forerunner of the modern concrete arch which now holds back the deep blue waters.

Today the lake is just one of many water projects in the state that serve such practical functions as generating electricity, irrigating crops, regulating spring runoff, and controlling against the dangers of storm-swollen floods. Nearly all these sites serve the happy secondary function of providing recreation, summer and winter. Deep-sea diving's out, but that's almost the only water-oriented recreation we don't indulge in here.

Jim Bones

Lit by the setting sun, a granite cliff casts its reflection in Nambé Lake in the Pecos Wilderness area of Santa Fe National Forest. Just south of 12,622-foot-high Santa Fe Baldy Peak, the small, remote alpine lake is one of six lakes in the 220,000-acre Pecos Wilderness. Lake Katherine, the "Queen of the Timberline," is especially popular with backpackers and wilderness goers.

Richard Bowman

Jim Bones

The Río Quemado Falls, "the best of the best" of New Mexico's waterfalls, located just inside the boundary of the Pecos Wilderness near the village of Truchas. Other popular New Mexico waterfalls include Sitting Bull Falls, about fifty miles southwest of Carlsbad in the foothills of the Guadalupe Mountains, and Bandelier National Monument's Frijoles Falls.

Photographers, nature lovers, and travelers at large tend to appreciate not only the cascading waterfalls, quiet pools, and splashing river rapids, but also the byproducts of water: the wildflowers that blossom in the meadows, forests, and prairies after a good rain; the water- and wind-sculpted sandstone and tuff; and the giant cottonwood trees and graceful tamarisks that line river banks, drawing nourishment from the water and standing out like beacons to signal its presence.

Because Indians, Spanish, and Anglos alike preferred to settle close to water, our waterways and water holes sometimes double as fragments from a history book. Like El Morro National Monument, where first Indian, then Spanish, and finally Anglo travelers carved inscriptions in the soft sandstone rock near the freshwater pool that lured them here. Or Villanueva State Park on the Pecos River, visited by Chamuscado, Coronado, Espejo, and other explorers as they searched for glory, lost friars, and gold. Or the Gila Cliff Dwellings National Monument north of Silver City on the west fork of the Gila River, where cliff dwelling members of the Mogollon culture lived for over a thousand years, farming beans, squash, and corn along the life-bringing stream. Or El Vado Lake on the Chama River, where the Old West town of El Vado once teemed with loggers, railroad workers, prostitutes, school marms, preachers of the Gospel, and even opera singers.

Indians, Hispanics, and Anglos in turn have all had a hand

Mike Schneps

in inventing colorful descriptive names for the waters of the state. Nambé Lake (and Nambé Creek and Nambé Falls) derive their name from a Tewa phrase, *nambay-ongwee,* meaning "the people of the roundish earth"—so named because of the ancient ruin mounds nearby. The Río Grande, the Big River, has also been called the Río de las Palmas (Palm Tree River), the Río Bravo (Wild River), and even the Río Turbio (Muddy River). And the waters of the Bottomless Lakes State Park bear names like the Devil's Inkwell, Mirror Lake, and Lazy Lagoon.

Our annual rainfall here is sparse, and in terms of things like million acre-feet of precipitation per year, this is clearly a water-poor land. Yet we're water-rich in the quality of our enjoyment of the stuff. And although we sometimes disagree about how to use this precious resource, or who's entitled to what percentage of which river, aquifer, lake, or stream, we do generally agree with the popular regional bumper-sticker slogan: *El Agua Es Vida.* Water is Life.

Dusk on the Gila River (left). Quiet, unspoiled, the Gila is a favorite river for canoeists, rafters, and kayakers who like their privacy. Canoeists report spending as long as two weeks on the water without encountering other river runners. Right, the Upper Nambé River meanders through the woods at 10,000 feet elevation in Santa Fe National Forest.

Jim Bones

Lee McAllister

Deep in the forest, a sparkling mountain stream brings life to plants and wild animals. In New Mexico you may have to climb to 6,000 feet or more to reach the point where the treeless plains give way to hills and trees. Even so, the state is thickly forested, with over nine million acres set aside as national forest. Wildlife abounds. At right, beaver-cut logs float near the headwaters of Costilla Creek in Taos County. Far right, the weathered remains of spruce and fir trees lie in the clear waters of Nambé Lake in the Sangre de Cristo Mountains. At high elevations, blue spruce and Douglas fir join the plentiful ponderosa pines.

24

Richard Bowman

Richard Bowman

The Jémez Falls, upper left, cascade down seventy rocky feet in the western part of the Santa Fe National Forest in Sandoval County. The forest service maintains an overlook of the falls for the benefit of photographers and other nature lovers. Lower left, the Pecos Falls descend step by step down the ancient rock. Deep in the heart of the Pecos Wilderness, these falls may be reached on horseback or foot.

Lee McAllister

Beautiful Nambé Lake in the Pecos Wilderness in Santa Fe National Forest. Over 1.4 million acres of New Mexico's national forests have been set aside in sixteen wilderness areas, from the Blue Range Wilderness in Apache National Forest in Catron County to the Wheeler Peak Wilderness in Taos County. The Gila Wilderness is the largest, with about 560,000 acres.

Mark Nohl

River rafters splash their way exuberantly down the Río Grande. The "Box," an eighteen-mile stretch of the river that cuts through the spectacular Río Grande Gorge, belongs to the national Wild and Scenic Rivers system. The Box challenges seasoned river runners with what river guides call "the toughest eighteen miles in America." Other, calmer stretches of the river allow beginners a chance to try their paddles in this burgeoning sport. Over a dozen outfitters offer river trips on the Río Grande and Río Chama, beginning in May and running some years as late as September.

Heron Lake, left, near Tierra Amarilla is a favorite with desert sailors because only trolling-speed motors are allowed. Sailboats slip gracefully across the waters of many of the more than twenty state lakes large enough for boating. Besides Heron, the most popular sailing lakes are Elephant Butte Lake near Truth or Consequences, Cochiti Lake near Cochiti Pueblo, and Navajo Lake near Aztec and Bloomfield. Below, river runners glide under the 650-foot-high Rio Grande Gorge Bridge on their way towards the next series of rapids.

Ken Gallard

Mark Nohl

David Ponton

*Left, motorboats on Elephant Butte Lake
in Elephant Butte State Park. Fishermen
angle year round in the nearly forty-mile-
long lake for catfish, bass, pike, and
crappie. Pelicans, sea gulls, and
abundant other wildlife also claim this
park as theirs. And in the ancient volcanic
ash beds adjoining the lake, rock hounds
and other explorers sometimes find fos-
silized wood and bits of dinosaur bones.
Above, a kayaker navigates in the white
water of the Río Grande near Pilar.
Right, wind surfers sail with the breeze
on Eagle Nest Lake northeast of Taos.*

Joe Hedrick

An Indian woman in colorful headdress performs the Rainbow Dance at Puyé Cliffs (above), ancestral home of the Santa Clara Pueblo Indians. The stone ruins of the ancient settlement survive on the mesa top near Española today. According to Santa Clara legend, drought drove their ancestors from the cliff-top homes to the riverside pueblo the Indians now occupy. Right, a handhewn Indian drum of aspen and rawhide. Indians around the state still make their own drums; best known are the drums from Cochiti Pueblo. The instruments are fashioned from hollowed aspen or cottonwood logs, which are dried slowly and peeled with handmade tools.

WITH BEAUTY BEFORE ME

The ten most beautiful women you could ever hope to see stand lined up in a row. They wear black overdresses, multi-colored underdresses, white moccasins, leggings, heavy woven red sashes, and a jewelry-store-load of turquoise and silver ornaments. Soon the drum begins beating and the women start to dance the *olla* or waterpot dance. Easily balancing exquisitely painted clay waterpots on their heads, the Olla "Maidens" (women in their fifties, sixties, and seventies) gracefully perform the ancient ritual steps of the Pueblo Indians.

Throughout the year Indians from the state's twenty-three pueblos and tribes perform ceremonies that date back a thousand—perhaps many thousand—years. Once regarded by outsiders as heathen rituals to be suppressed at all costs, Indian ceremonial dances of New Mexico today draw sightseers and anthropologists from all over the globe. The drumbeat begins. The low chanting in Tewa, Tiwa, Towa, Keresan, Zuni, or Athabascan rises and falls; and the dancers and the watching crowd find themselves transported into another time and place, another way of looking at the world. The sacred cycle of the corn plant unfolds. The mystical union between Mother Earth and Father Sky becomes clear. The meaning of the Navajo chant lingers after the words die: *With beauty before me as I walk. With beauty before me as I walk. With beauty before me as I walk.*

All twenty-three tribes except the Mescalero Apaches and the Alamo band of the Navajos live in the northern half of the state. Descendants of brilliant warriors whose skill as guerrilla fighters survives in legend and song still, the Mescaleros today are known largely for the panoramic 460,000 acres of New Mexico's highlands which are now their tribal home—and which they generously share with outsiders. Hunters, fishermen, skiers, and wildflower lovers flock to this mountain paradise, which includes the Sierra Blanca ski area and the Inn of the Mountain Gods. A highlight of the Mescalero year comes early in July, when Indians and non-Indians gather for the dramatic Apache Maidens' Puberty Rites ceremonial, which lasts four days and includes dawn rituals and a nighttime Mountain Spirits Dance around a blazing fire. In the north, the Mescaleros' cultural cousins, the Jicarilla Apaches, perform similar rites in July.

Nowhere else in the United States have so many ancient Indian rituals, so much ancient Indian thought, so many ancient Indian customs survived as here in New Mexico. The Navajos, concentrated in the northwest corner of New Mexico and the northeast portion of Arizona after migrating here six centuries or more ago, still belong to poetically named clans like the Salt Clan and the Bitter-Water Clan. They still build—and still live in—earth and log hogans with the doorway facing east to greet the rising sun. They still talk of the five worlds that have been (we live now in the "World of Changing Color") and the two worlds which are yet to come. And they still perform the chantway rituals of blessing, purification, and healing

Richard C. Sandoval

in the privacy of their family groups and clans.

In villages along the Río Grande, and in two lines extending west—one up towards the Jémez Mountains, the other due west towards Zuni land—the nineteen Pueblo tribes live in or near ancient settlements or "pueblos" dating back to the great migrations of the twelfth and thirteenth centuries. Taos Pueblo with its many-storied adobe residences and Acoma, the "Sky City" on a mesa top, are considered the most visually striking. But whether they occupy the adobe and stone houses of their ancestors or modern dwellings that look like Anywhere, U.S.A., or something in between, the Pueblo Indians still retain many of their ancient beliefs and customs. They still classify themselves as Summer People (Squash People) and Winter People (Turquoise People). They still belong to curing, hunting, warrior, rain, and fertility societies. They still maintain and use their sacred ceremonial kivas, which hark all the way back to the first few centuries A.D., to the days when the Basketmaker ancestors of modern Pueblo Indians lived in pithouses.

Even though they may be prosperous, high-powered businessmen and women during the ordinary workaday world, they still discard their three-piece suits, paint their faces blue and red, daub their bodies with mud, and wrap themselves with evergreen boughs and

Deer dancers at Santa Clara Pueblo, above, and buffalo dancers, right. Colorfully garbed dancers perform thirty or more animal dances in New Mexico's pueblos throughout the year, including the buffalo, deer, elk, and sacred ram dances. The ritual steps, gestures, and calls emphasize the link between animals and humans, a bond which remains strong in the Pueblo view of the world today despite centuries of outside cultural influences. Sometimes friendly competition exists between pueblos. Santa Clara deer dancers perform superbly, but Indians from nearby San Juan Pueblo will tell you laughingly that their deer dance is even better.

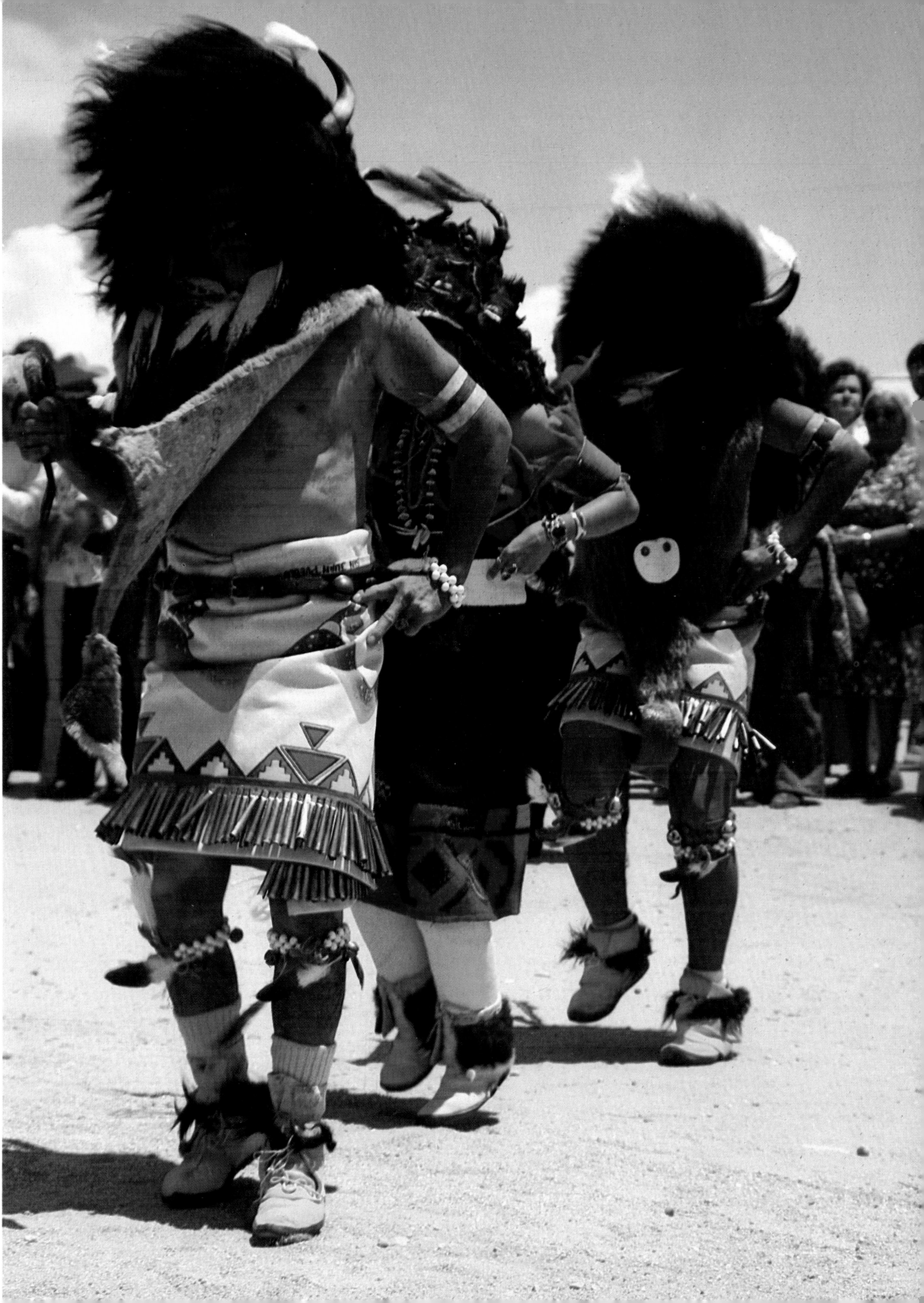

Joe Hill

Joe Hedrick

colorful tribal garb to participate in the ancient dances: the animal dances and corn dances, the butterfly dances and cloud dances, the snowbird and feather dances, and many more. They may know the latest in twentieth-century hi-tech jargon, but certain specially designated medicine people are still bound by custom and conscience to return to the pueblo by sunset each day—for life.

Over the centuries New Mexico's Indians have learned to be cautious in trusting non-Indians with many of the details of their beliefs and ways. Much of what transpires on the pueblos and in the kivas is private, not available for the inspection of the evangelizing, analyzing, scrutinizing Western mind. However, museums (primarily in Albuquerque, in Santa Fe, and at tribal locations) and visitor centers at places like Salmon Ruins, Aztec National Monument, Chaco Culture National Historical Park, Bandelier National Monument, and Salinas National Monument offer insights into the culture of

Harvest dancers at Santa Clara Pueblo (above) and the Buffalo Mother at a Buffalo Dance at Santa Clara (right). Traditionally, the Buffalo Mother wears a sun symbol on her back. As the metaphorical mother of all larger animals, she leaves the pueblo at dawn and returns leading them. Properly performed, Pueblo dances and ceremonials are believed to ensure the smooth continuity of the natural cycle of the earth and all life. Many rituals are considered sacred, and most pueblos prohibit or restrict photography.

Joe Hedrick

Left, the Basket Dance at San Juan Pueblo north of Española. At nearby San Ildefonso Pueblo, dancers often perform the basket dance at Easter, a high point in the Pueblo ceremonial year dating back to ancient celebrations of the coming of spring. The festivities typically begin on Easter Sunday and continue several days. Colorful drums, below, boom steadily throughout the dances. The annual Inter-Tribal Indian Ceremonial in Gallup, the Indian Pueblo Cultural Center in Albuquerque, and the Indian Market in Santa Fe all feature off-reservation dance performances.

Mark Nohl

New Mexico's Indians, present and past. Likewise, the carefully crafted jewelry and the intricate clay pottery, which varies in design and execution from tribe to tribe, often give a sense of indirect participation in another culture's beliefs and ways. Raindrops, mountains, lightning, heart lines, kiva steps, bear claws, water serpents, feathers, melons, deer, and other stylized symbols decorate pots and provide jewelry design.

Above all, the ceremonials, particularly at Christmas, New Year's, Easter, and each pueblo's patron saint day, provide an unforgettable glimpse into this very different way of life. At the 1984 Inter-Tribal Indian Ceremonial held in Gallup in August, a small Anglo boy turned to his mother and asked, "But 'cept, what *is* a ceremonial, Mom?"

A ceremonial is a doorway to another world.

Russell Bamert

The gold of transformed aspen trees (right) and cottonwoods dominates New Mexico's autumn. But the red leaves of a rare stand of maples (above) paint autumn scarlet on the eastern slopes of the Manzano Mountains, near the picturesque Turquoise Trail villages of Tajique and Torreón on NM 14. In the southern part of the state the Guadalupe Mountains also harbor maples.

AUTUMN'S GLOW

The clear air grows clearer, the blue sky bluer, and even in the sunshine the breeze blows cool. The neighbors begin hauling home firewood in their pickups. Chile ristras appear. Breakfasts on the patio are just a memory, and the light blanket that kept you warm at night all summer would leave you shivering now. Autumn's here—time to pick up your camera, your sketchpad, your notebook of poems, and linger outside, where nature's alchemy is transforming the green world to gold.

In the mountains the first signs of autumn arrive early. A wild strawberry plant that exchanges its green leaves for red. Wild grasses that turn yellow and orange. Then suddenly a forest full of aspen trees that glow gold in the sun. An occasional maple tree that turns bright red. Half the state seems to head for the mountain roads, with the idea of experiencing—and recording—this magical season. Depending on the weather and the year, the "aspencade" caravans (structured and unstructured tours of aspen country that range from family-planned outings to tour groups) begin in mid to late September and continue as long as a month.

Meanwhile, as if to remind the world of their existence, the valleys are preparing their counterpoint response. The cottonwood trees lining riverbanks and streams, or signaling a wet spot on an otherwise dry plain, begin to turn yellow and orange, first upriver—or *río arriba,* as it's often called here—then *río abajo,* downriver, too.

While some of us are out admiring golden aspens and cottonwoods, others are busy with the harvest. Beans, corn, and squash thrive here, just as they did a thousand years ago. So does the legendary chile plant, with each region's farmers ending the season by debating the merits of the variety they've raised. Special growing techniques can sometimes change the taste of pungent varieties of chile from mild (that's relatively speaking) to very hot (nothing relative about that at all). As gardeners and small farmers harvest their pumpkins, grapes, onions, apples, and melons, agribusiness ventures supervise the gathering of another huge harvest of cotton, the state's number one crop.

Autumn's also a time when the whole state seems to be in motion. There are fairs to attend, fiestas to participate in, hot air balloon festivals and rallies, foot races to run, concerts to listen to, plays to watch. In the mountains of the north, lumberjacks and jills gather in Angel Fire Labor Day weekend for the annual Paul Bunyan Days celebrations, with events like logrolling and woodcutting competitions. Starting in Red River, six hundred bicyclists or so pedal off in September on the Enchanted Circle Wheeler Peak Century Tour. The hundred-mile course climbs thousands of feet over steep mountain roads that can make even the heartiest cyclist start thinking about getting into better shape.

As September ends and October begins, Red River hosts a two-weekend aspencade festival that includes square dancing contests as well as colored leaves. Angel Fire and Cloudcroft combine an

40

Richard C. Sandoval

Richard C. Sandoval

Left, a wild sunflower glows in the autumn sun. Right, strands of red chile, called "ristras," dry in the sun near Velarde, an agricultural village in Río Arriba County along the northern Río Grande. Gradually the ristra grows shorter as the shiny dried chiles, a basic ingredient in many New Mexican dishes, find their way into the family cooking pot.

Oktoberfest with their aspencade tours of the foliage. From Alamogordo a different sort of car caravan sets out, one day early each autumn, for the once-a-year-only tour of the Trinity Site, location of the first atomic bomb explosion, in 1945. Albuquerque rings with the sounds of rapidly spoken Greek at the annual October Grecian Festival sponsored by St. George Greek Orthodox Church; and Carlsbad, famous for its nearby caverns and their bats, hosts a 16 de Septiembre fiesta, commemorating the famed *Grito de Dolores* (cry of anguish) speech that led to Mexico's independence from Spain. At about the same time (the first weekend after Labor Day) revelers in Santa Fe are celebrating the Fiesta de Santa Fe, considered the oldest ongoing community celebration in the United States. Among other things, it commemorates the Spanish return to New Mexico in 1692-93, a dozen years after the Pueblo Revolt of 1680.

Art exhibits, always a major part of the state's cultural offerings and one of the enrichers of its economy, blossom around the state in the fall like late-season wildflowers—and not just in the art centers of Santa Fe and Taos or in conjunction with aspencade events. Hillsboro, east of Silver City, hosts an annual Black Range Artists Show at its yearly Hillsboro Apple Festival early in September. At Gallup, an international trade center for Indian jewelry and art, the Gallup Area Arts Council sponsors an arts and crafts show of both Indian and non-Indian arts and crafts. The arts council in Artesia, the "Heart of the Pecos Valley" between Roswell and Carlsbad, reminds the world through its October exhibits that art can thrive in the flatlands, too.

Visitors who trek to Santa Fe to attend the annual Festival of the Arts in late October may find the city still autumn crisp and colorful, or lying already under winter's first offering of snow. But until that first snow falls—and sometimes even after that—the autumn bustle in New Mexico continues. And why not? It's worth a little early morning chilliness to come out in the predawn darkness and marvel at the sight of five hundred colorful hot air balloons rising into the morning sky over Albuquerque, or the even crisper feeling in the air, about November first, as many of the same balloons ascend against the blue sky of Taos.

It's worth braving the tingling chill of a November night to attend a performance of the New Mexico Symphony Orchestra or the fall concert of the Orchestra of Santa Fe. And throughout New Mexico as the cold weather spreads, there's the joy of Thanksgiving, when the harvest is in and the season's done, and offerings of thanks rise in various languages for the gift of a New Mexico autumn and the bounty it brings.

An autumn vista in the Sangre de Cristo Mountains. Each autumn the forests fill with photographers and sightseers taking "aspencade" tours of the fall foliage. Favorite aspencade areas include the Sacramento and White mountains of the south, the Sangre de Cristo and Jémez mountains of the north, and the Gila National Forest in the southwest. The Cumbres and Toltec Scenic Railroad (p. 82) also winds through aspencade country.

Lee McAllister

A small cottonwood gleams among the glistening gypsum sands of White Sands National Monument. The shrub-like tree lives in a transition zone where the sands are stable enough to support some life. In the heart of the 230-square-mile monument, the constantly shifting dunes are nearly vegetation free; but beetles, lizards, birds, and other creatures all leave their soft prints in the sand. Sunset or a rising full moon transforms the flowing dunes into a photographer's wonderland.

Jeff Gladfelter

Glowing autumn leaves in the Sandía Mountains along La Luz Trail, right.

Jonathan Meyers

Richard C. Sandoval

On the banks of the Río Grande south of Las Cruces, a cottonwood glows orange-gold in the late afternoon light, left. The fast-growing Río Grande cottonwood, known for centuries simply as "el alamo," sometimes reaches a height of 100 feet. Around the state street names like Alameda, Alamosa, and Alamo attest to the presence and importance of this ancient friend of the shade- and water-seeking traveler. Above, the ubiquitous chamisa, an evergreen shrub that saves its bright yellow blossoms for fall.

Aspen leaves blanket a trail in Santa Fe National Forest (right). Throughout the state, autumn is a favorite season for short backcountry hikes. Longer excursions require careful planning— early autumn snows can turn a fall outing into a winter camping trip.

Jeff Glickman

Russell Bamert

*Early autumn brings cooler air—
and regional fairs. Here,
youngsters squeal as they zoom
along on the roller coaster at the
New Mexico State Fair, held in
Albuquerque in September. The
sprawling fair boasts all the
standard state fair trappings, plus
special Spanish and Indian villages
and an annual Sheep-to-Shawl
weaving exhibit. The fun dates
back to 1881, when the New
Mexico Territorial Fair was born,
thirty-one years before New Mexico
became a state. Other popular
fairs include the Curry County
Fair in Clovis, largest county fair
in the Southwest; the Eastern New
Mexico State Fair in Roswell; and
the Southwest New Mexico State
Fair in Deming. Straddling the
Arizona-New Mexico state line,
Navajoland's capital city of
Window Rock (Tségháhoodzání)
hosts the colorful Navajo Nation
Tribal Fair each September.*

Russell Bamert

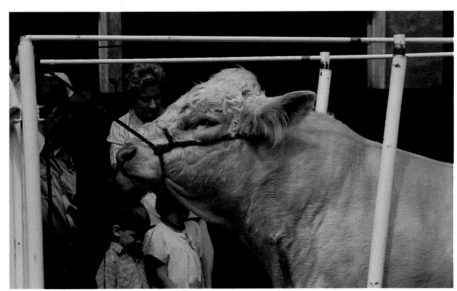

Richard C. Sandoval

No, folks. We don't typically make our enchiladas the size of the one above. But at the annual Whole Enchilada Fiesta in Las Cruces the first weekend in October, the world's largest enchilada is born—along with more moderately sized burritos, tamales, tacos, tostadas compuestas, and such. For those with a lighter appetite, there's Indian fry bread or fresh corn on the cob. In nearby Hatch, September's annual Chile Festival honors the fiery chile. Left, champion livestock such as this fill regional fairs and play an important role in the state's economy. "Cattle-guard" may be a ranch child's first spoken word.

48

Richard C. Sandoval

A traditional painted wooden santo (saint) at Albuquerque's annual Feria Artesana in late August, left. Weaving, tinworking, woodcarving, straw inlay, colcha embroidery, and other traditional Hispanic crafts flourish in New Mexico. The Spanish Market in Santa Fe, held late in July, also provides a showcase for New Mexico's Hispanic craftspeople. Below, an Indian woman sells pottery at Santa Fe's annual Indian Market in August, which draws prominent Indian artists and artisans from around the country. The Eight Northern Indian Pueblos also sponsor a popular arts and crafts show each July featuring the work of Indian craftspeople from many tribes. Below left, on the pleasant grounds of the Shidoni Foundry and Gallery in Tesuque, north of Santa Fe, where sculptors from around the world show their work. Lavishly costumed performers at the Santa Fe Opera (above right) and the Albuquerque Civic Light Opera (below right). Founded in 1957, the Santa Fe Opera presents a two-month summer season that includes both well-known operas like The Magic Flute and little-known but engaging pieces like Richard Strauss's Intermezzo.

Richard C. Sandoval

At sunrise about five hundred hot air balloons ascend to fill the morning sky at Albuquerque's annual International Balloon Fiesta in early autumn (above left). Farmington, Angel Fire, Taos, and Santa Fe also host yearly balloon fiestas; and the graceful hot air globes appear at events like Clovis's Pioneer Days in June and Gallup's Inter-Tribal Indian Ceremonial in August. Right, a balloon floats upward, allowing passengers to savor the early morning landscape and the fresh breeze. Below left, a rocket from the Apollo Project juts into the clear air outside the International Space Hall of Fame in Alamogordo's popular Space Center. The center also features laser shows, an Omnifax Theater, and dramatic recreations of celestial events.

David Ponton

A snow and frost-painted pine bough in the Jémez Mountains (above) and a snowy winter scene in the Sangre de Cristo Mountains (right), both in the Santa Fe National Forest. With more than 120 mountain peaks topping 10,000 feet in elevation and about 10,000 square miles of snowy winter terrain, New Mexico in winter is a haven for artists, photographers, nature lovers, and winter sports enthusiasts.

THE SPARKLE OF WINTER

In the backcountry villages of the state of Maine, old-timers sometimes laugh about how there are only two seasons in those parts: July and winter. In New Mexico at high elevations the same joke brings a laugh of recognition.

It's no more true here than it is there, of course, but a truth lies behind the wit. From about 7,000 feet elevation and up, winters in New Mexico are long, and the higher you climb, the snowier it gets. Even at 7,000 feet the local weather wisdom insists that it "always" snows before Halloween, and it may snow in May. That snow makes New Mexico at higher altitudes a magnet for winter sports lovers. From December through March about 10,000 square miles of the state often lie buried in snow, which nature tops obligingly and frequently (especially at high elevations) with downy powder. Average annual snowfall in the highlands is over 100 inches, and up to 600 inches of snow sometimes falls in the mountains of the north.

That's a lot of snow—enough to spend a long time gliding quietly along through the wilderness on cross-country skis, discovering the world of the forest and meadow winter. About 5,000 square miles of New Mexico's snow-covered terrain make excellent cross-country skiing. Much of that lies in the wilderness and national forest areas.

The hardest part of a cross-country skiing trip in New Mexico may be in deciding where to go. Shall it be on one of the trails along Hyde Park in the Santa Fe National Forest, handy to the capital and after-ski amenities? Shall it be into the remote Wheeler Peak Wilderness area northeast of Taos, which provides what some Nordic skiers call "the most dramatic ski touring" in New Mexico—with the drama including avalanche risk? How about out in the majestic snowfields surrounding Truchas Peaks, or perhaps over in the Jémez country, where steaming natural hot springs in the forest tempt skiers away from their skis. Or maybe down in the high country of the Gila Wilderness, about which even writers of ski manuals say simply, "Let us know what you find."

The same potential dilemma confronts the downhill skier. Which of the state's ten commercial ski areas will it be? Taos Ski Valley, of course, is the best known, famous nationally and internationally for its heart-stopping vertical inclines for advanced and expert skiers (but "we have beginner slopes, too," the signs reassure). Adding to the lure at Taos are the guaranteed-short lift lines, the low-key no-nonsense approach to ski slopes, and—above all—the legendary man who's been running the show since the slopes opened in 1955 at the site of an old gold-mining camp.

But Taos is only one option. Skiers swoosh happily down beginning, intermediate, and advanced slopes at each of the other commercial skiing areas. Besides Taos, there's Angel Fire, Cloudcroft, Red River, Río Costilla, Sandía Peak, Santa Fe, Sierra Blanca, Sipapu, and Sugarite, with other ski centers appearing and disappearing from time to time. Strung like a belt down the center of the state in a 350-mile range from north to south, the skiing areas often lie close

Sunlight brightens the forest on a winter day in the Sandía Mountains. The Sandía Peak area includes some of the best Nordic ski trails in the state. Most of the Alpine runs are for intermediate skiers, and the peak's a favorite skiing site for telemarkers. It's also a handy backyard playground for the citizens of Albuquerque, the state's only real metropolis. But cross-country skiers in search of solitude may still find it in the Sandía Mountain Wilderness area of Cíbola National Forest or the nearby Manzano Mountain Wilderness.

Right, wooden and stone markers at the camposanto, *the village cemetery outside the church at Cañoncito at Apache Canyon. This historic village was once the last station on the Santa Fe Trail before reaching Santa Fe.*

Betty Adams

Tom Smylie

to sightseeing attractions. Skiers at Taos Ski Valley may take an afternoon off to browse through the art galleries and shops of the nearby town of Taos. Snow bunnies at Sugarite may take a quick detour over to Capulín Mountain National Monument, site of an ancient volcanic cinder cone. Skiers in the south, in Cloudcroft or Sierra Blanca, can easily combine their skiing with a visit to the famous White Sands in the Tularosa Valley below the snowy mountains. And visitors to Santa Fe or Albuquerque sometimes work their business or sightseeing schedules around a few runs down the ski slopes in either city's backyard.

Of course, we're no more a one-sport state in the winter than any other time of the year. Plenty of people here who love the winter outdoors never attach their feet to skis. Instead, they snowshoe, snow camp, snow mobile, ice fish, or toboggan. Some even slide across the snow yelling "Mush!" to the team of Siberian Huskies pulling them and their sleds.

For many, winter's a time to stay close to home and admire the ice in the backyard pond or the frost that sometimes paints windows here like they used to be painted, early mornings, when your grandpa—or you—were a kid. Winter's a time to sit in front of a gracefully arched kiva fireplace and warm yourself in the glow of burning pine or piñon. A time to look out in the early evening and watch the sky turn red with the sunset. To take a walk around the block and savor the feel of that cold, crisp, pure air, perfumed with the scent of burning piñon.

But of course, all that's at high altitudes, relatively speaking. Below 7,000-7,500 feet even cross-country skiers are usually hard put to find more than a rapidly melting patch of snow, except during or just after a storm.

How do all those New Mexicans who live at lower elevations

56 (and that's much of the population) get along with winters of infrequent or fast-melting snow? Well, down below 4,000 feet, in places like Carlsbad, Las Cruces, Artesia, and Hobbs, they'll tell you it feels pretty nice to be warm when the rest of the country's cold, to watch that January thermometer climb into the fifties day after day—and not just because of a January thaw. In fact, you might even hear them chuckling down there about how there are really only two seasons in those parts: spring and July.

Jeff Gladfelter

Above, pristine snowfields in the Sangre de Cristo Mountains above the Santa Fe Ski Basin. The popular ski area, with over thirty Alpine runs about equally divided between beginner, intermediate, and advanced, lies just sixteen miles northeast of the almost 400-year-old state capital. Après-ski activities here include afternoon visits to museums and art galleries, and quiet strolls through winding, snow-covered lanes. Right, winter in the Jémez Mountains, where meadows, woodlands, natural hot springs, and good snowfalls combine to make this a cross-country skiers' favorite.

David Ponton

58

Mark Nohl

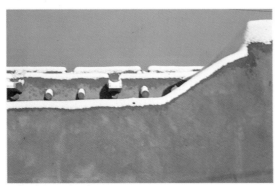

Richard C. Sandoval

The camposanto outside the High Road Village of Truchas, with panoramic Truchas Peaks looming towards the sky. Winter or summer, the High Road to Taos from Santa Fe offers a scenic alternate route through centuries-old Hispanic villages where Hispanic traditions and folk arts thrive. Left, snow outlines the roof of an adobe building in Santa Fe. Right, the snow-covered Sangre de Cristo Mountains, where the first snow of the season may fall in September, and the last snow flurry fly in June.

Mark Nohl

Skiers glide upslope in a cozy gondola at the Sierra Blanca Ski Area near Ruidoso in the southern part of the state (above left). Sierra Blanca Peak, at an altitude of 12,003 feet, is the highest point in southern New Mexico, and snowfalls are heavy here—an average of nearly 200 inches a year. The Mescalero Apache Tribe owns this popular ski area and the nearby Inn of the Mountain Gods. Right, and below left, Alpine skiers enjoy the fine powder snow at famed Taos Ski Valley, where over half of the approximately seventy runs are for advanced and expert skiers.

Ken Gallard

Ken Gallard

The fifty-passenger red and blue tram cars of Sandía Peak Tram Company (left) transport skiers and sightseers from Albuquerque to Sandía Peak, a dramatic 2.7-mile voyage that covers 3,819 vertical feet in 18 minutes. NO, you may NOT ride outside. That's the tram manager there, making the daily early-morning inspection run. Above, a cross-country skier glides easily across the snow in the Taos Ski Valley, renowned for its downhill skiing, but becoming increasingly popular with cross-country skiers addicted to the joys of winter exploration.

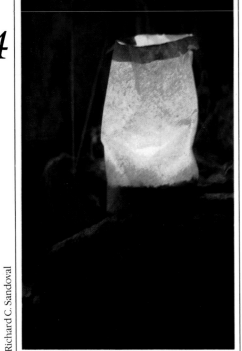

The December night glows with the twinkling lights of farolitos *(above, and right). A Spanish word meaning "little lanterns," farolitos are known as* luminarias *south of Santa Fe. To confuse matters, the popular bonfires lighting the pathway for Christmas processions are called luminarias in the north.*

FELIZ NAVIDAD

Feliz Navidad! Merry Christmas! It's Christmas Eve, and across New Mexico doorbells are ringing as *primos, tíos, hermanos, y toda la familia*—cousins, aunts, uncles, brothers, sisters, the entire family—gather to celebrate *la Noche Buena,* Christmas Eve. Soon the extended family will collect around the heavily laden table and spill over into the rest of the house as they eat homemade tortillas and sopaipillas, posole and natillas, empanaditas and enchiladas, bizcochitos and tamales: spicy, mouth-watering foods and sweet desserts.

Tonight even the young family members who seldom speak Spanish may spend the evening laughing and chattering in a rapid-fire blend of Spanish and English that changes back and forth so quickly from one language to the other that neither speaker nor listener notices. While *los viejitos* (the old folks) talk of lean Christmases past, *los niños,* the children, may chime in. "No te olvides, you said we could abrir our presents esta noche, Dad." (Or conversely, "Don't forget, dijiste que podemos open los regalos tonight, Papá.)

As with practically everything else in the state, people celebrate the holidays here in many different ways—with German, French, Jewish, Indian, and old-fashioned Middle America customs, including the twinkle of electric Christmas lights. But the glow of the season for many New Mexicans begins with the *farolitos* (as they're called from Santa Fe north) or *luminarias* (as they're known in most of the rest of the state). The components are simple: candles, sand, and paper bags. Put them together, and the yellow light of the candles shining out through sand-weighted paper bags brings a romantic softness to the night that makes colored electric lights seem a little garish by comparison.

Good food, family gatherings, the friendly buzz of Spanish, and the gentle flames of farolitos/luminarias are only part of what makes a New Mexican Hispanic Christmas different from Christmases in most other areas of the country. At the heart of a traditional Christmas here are processions, pageants, medieval mystery plays, and colorful dances connected to the days of the Moorish invasion of Spain.

For many, the holidays begin on or just before December 12, Our Lady of Guadalupe's Day, when festivity and ritual lovers join worshipers in candlelight processions through the often frosty night. Bonfires light the way. Traffic stops, as the parade of well-bundled celebrants passes through the streets commemorating the legend of the appearance of Nuestra Señora de Guadalupe, Our Lady of Guadalupe, to a poor Indian man named Juan Diego in Mexico in December 1531.

Then on December 16, the nine-day celebration of *Las Posadas* begins. (La posada means "the inn.") From the villages of the north to the barrio neighborhoods of the south, New Mexicans turn out to reenact the Biblical story of Mary and Joseph (María y José) searching for a place to spend the night. Again and again, the cold, tired couple begs to be allowed to enter. Again and again, admission is denied. Finally the doors open. A place has been found for the

Lining rooftops and sidewalks, farolitos transform the winter night throughout New Mexico. Mark Nohl

Mark Nohl

Santo Niño, the Christ Child, to be born.

Other pageants, like this, date back to the medieval mystery plays of Europe. *Los Pastores* retells the story of the shepherds tending their flocks. *Los Tres Reyes Magos* relives the coming of the Magi. Adding color to the season and the ritualized dramas, the carefully arranged *nacimientos* (Nativity scenes) depict Baby Jesus—often an Indian or Hispanic Baby Jesus—in a manger. Sometimes out in the countryside the stable of the nacimiento stirs with the movements of live animals chosen to help portray that eventful Noche Buena long ago.

In traditional celebrations, all morning long on Christmas Day children go door to door singing and collecting token gifts. And Christmas day sometimes still throbs with the dancing of the Matachines, a colorful ritual which began in Africa unknown centuries ago and came with the Moors to Spain. The dance arrived in New Mexico with the early Spanish colonists and now is more frequently performed by New Mexico's Indians than by Hispanics.

That seems appropriate somehow. Just as it seems natural that farolitos (or luminarias) are often more ardently displayed by Anglos and non-native New Mexicans than by those who developed them historically. Once it's clearly understood that we all have a right to maintain our separate cultural heritages and ways of doing things here, we rather enjoy borrowing from and sharing customs with our neighbors. You may never have sung a Spanish Christmas carol in your life. Almost certainly, you'll never be forced to sing one here. But once it's understood that you're completely free to choose, you may find yourself impatiently waiting for the special Christmas Eve gathering at the *Misa del Gallo,* the midnight "Rooster's

According to legend, the custom of lighting farolitos goes back to the days of early Spanish exploration, when the Spanish reached the Philippines and encountered Chinese paper lanterns. The explorers admired the festive lights and brought some back with them when they returned to the Americas.

Mass," and the singing of the traditional *villancico* (carol):

> *Vamos todos a Belén*
> *Con amor y gozo*
> *Adoremos al Señor*
> *Nuestro Redentor.*

> Let's all go to Bethlehem
> Lovingly, with pleasure.
> Let's adore the Lord,
> Our Savior.

No matter where or how you celebrate the holidays, our wish for you is still the same: *Feliz Navidad, y Prospero Año Nuevo.* Merry Christmas, and a Prosperous New Year.

The Church of San Francisco de Asís at Ranchos de Taos in northern New Mexico. Down in Tularosa, in the southern part of the state, the Church of San Francisco de Paula and the surrounding streets also glow with the lights of these special New Mexico Christmas illuminations.

Greg Martin

Mark Nohl

Above, a reenactment of Las Posadas, *in which María and José (Mary and Joseph) seek a place to stay in the crowded city of Belén (Bethlehem). Below,* Los Pastores, *the story of the shepherds who came to see Jesús.*

Mark Nohl

Bob Caspar

*The Plaza of Albuquerque's Old Town on a
winter night (right). Christmas in New Mexico
is seldom snowy below 6,500 feet elevation,
but it's still a joyous time of year. For many
New Mexicans the Christmas season lasts from
December 12, Guadalupe's Day, to January 6,
El Día de los Tres Reyes Magos (Epiphany).*

Mark Nohl

Pilgrims in a candlelight procession reach the Cross of the Martyrs on a cool September evening in Santa Fe. The procession concludes the annual Fiesta de Santa Fe, considered to be the oldest ongoing community festivities in the United States today. The first fiesta was celebrated in September 1712 as a day of thanksgiving for the safe return of the Spanish to New Mexico in the 1690s, following the Pueblo Revolt of 1680. The proclamation establishing the new holiday ordered that it be celebrated yearly "forever." Right, a woman from Isleta Pueblo, south of Albuquerque, carries a basket full of fresh bread. Still baked outdoors in the traditional beehive-shaped hornos *(ovens), Indian bread is a popular component of New Mexican cuisine.*

LA GENTE: THE PEOPLE

T he man in the department store stands in front of a rack of boys' winter jackets trying to decide whether to buy a blue one or a green one for his young son. He turns and says something to the boy, and they both laugh.

What did he say? You won't know unless you speak Zuni, the ancient language of the people of Zuni Pueblo.

All around New Mexico scenes and events that appear perfectly ordinary at first, typical-anywhere-U.S.A., have a way of taking on an unexpected flavor. That's partly because, among our 1.4 million inhabitants, we have such a diverse cultural mix . . . descendants of the early Athabascan Indians who moved into this region six centuries ago, and descendants of the Anasazi Indians, who thrived in New Mexico a thousand years ago . . . descendants of the conquistadores, who still preserve much of their ancient tradition and lore . . . descendants of the early Anglo trappers and traders and pioneers, who arrived here via the Santa Fe Trail in the north and across the Llano Estacado in the south, seeking space and a place to put down roots . . . descendants of those who came by train from the East after 1880, seeking—and finding—health. And a whole lot of people from all over, who've discovered in this century that New Mexico seems to strike some kind of responsive chord in them that makes them want to stay.

And they do, in growing numbers. From 1970 to 1980, New Mexico gained 287,000 people, an increase of 28 percent.

Even so, we are largely a rural state: about 25 percent of us still live in rural areas, and approximately another 25 percent live in communities of under 25,000. Yet almost two-thirds of the remainder live in one small county, near the heart of the state, in the Albuquerque metropolitan area.

Since New Mexico ranks only forty-one in the United States by per capita personal income, it's clearly not usually money that draws people here, or keeps them here. But for whatever reason they originally come, it's the people, some say, who constitute the real wealth of this state. And they all have a story to tell, or many stories to tell, if you're patient and know how to wait.

Take someone like Bill, who was born down in Mountain Park, near Alamogordo, in 1921. With typical New Mexico get-up-and-go gumption, the tattered looking kid from the farm decided he'd grow up to be a famous cartoonist. And he did. Today you might run into renowned political cartoonist Bill Mauldin buying a paper in a country store in Mountain Park, where he's traveled from his home in northern New Mexico down to visit his mother and brother, who still live on the old family farm.

Or people like Orlando, whose ancestors arrived here in 1598 and put down such strong roots in northern New Mexico that the family has lived in the villages along the High Road to Taos ever since. Today you might meet Orlando Romero at the History Library of the Museum of New Mexico in Santa Fe, where he spends his

Left, colorfully dressed charros (horsemen) *from the* Asociación de Charros en la Capital de Santa Fe *in a* charreada *competition. Above right, outside the post office in Terrero (the official spelling of this name changes periodically; the unofficial spelling changes all the time) on the upper Pecos River north of the villages of Rowe and Pecos. In small towns the post office is still a favorite community gathering place. Lower right, in the Río Hondo area near the village of Lincoln, where the grandparents of today's old-timers once sheltered famous outlaw Billy the Kid. On April 28, 1881, the Kid made his famous jailbreak from the Lincoln County Courthouse. Today the courthouse and many of the other old buildings in town, including the authentically restored Wortley Hotel, are part of the New Mexico state monument system.*

Mark Nohl

days helping people explore the details of New Mexico's past.

Or someone like Peggy W., who grew up in Boston, but moved to Las Cruces, and fell so much in love with New Mexico that she couldn't leave. Oh, she tried, once or twice, but each time something about the people and the place lured her back.

Or a woman like Susie Wood, a Navajo Indian who lives in Gallup and weaves "Two-Gray-Hill" rugs and other traditional designs using natural wools and dies. At home the family raises sheep, whose wool Susie washes, cards, dyes, and spins, before weaving it the way her two grandmothers taught her to when she was still a child.

Or people who can spin yarns and tell tales. People who'll explain to you how Maljamar, off in Lea County, got its name, and why the windmill in Rodeo, down in Hidalgo County, is painted a bright turquoise blue. Or the story of Billy the Kid, Vicente Silva, Elfego Baca, or the Lincoln County War.

And even just grocery shopping some night, you may encounter the unexpected. The person standing in line behind you might be the governor of the state, or the executive director of the Eight Northern Indian Pueblos Council,

Buddy Mays

Buddy Mays

or the Archbishop. She might be a *curandera*, versed in the use of ancient Indian and Hispanic herbal medicines; or an *enjarradora*, a woman who adds the mud plaster to the outside of adobe buildings in a tradition dating back hundreds—perhaps thousands—of years; or the head of her own company, or a famous artist, or the secretary of state.

Or it might be someone not famous at all, except to the children or grandchildren of the family, who like to hear stories about how things used to be. About how in the summer on a Sunday afternoon people would sit out in the shade of the porch or under a cottonwood tree by a stream, laughing and talking and passing the day. About winter evenings before electricity came in, not so long ago, and the neighbors would gather by the fire to laugh and tell stories until late in the winter night, when the embers died, the children fell asleep, the storytelling dwindled, and the neighbors all walked home.

A Hispanic weaver at her loom. Centuries-old Hispanic folk arts thrive in New Mexico today, and many weavers live and work in the historic Hispanic villages north of Santa Fe, some of which were first established nearly four centuries ago. Natural dyes are still used to produce the soft earth tones, rusts, and rich indigos that characterize many of the traditional weavings. Designs are typically geometric or abstract.

Johnnie Martinez

A cattleman tinkers with a windmill along the Pecos River. Windmills dot the hills and plains, providing the energy to draw water for livestock. Today most ranches run only a few thousand acres each, but legendary cattlemen of an earlier era—scoundrel-heroes like John Chisum and Albert B. Fall—once owned huge spreads. Fall's ranch included 750,000 acres of grazing land.

Buddy Mays

Left, a young woman from Santa Clara Pueblo, dressed in traditional ceremonial garb. Right, a woman from the Pecos region. Historically, life along the Pecos has sometimes been a struggle for the salt-of-the-earth people who live there, but a strong sense of heritage and the beauty of the river and the region have kept the same families there for generations. Below, a child at the historic Río Feliz Ranch near Lincoln. Known today as the Flying H, the ranch and its owners played prominent roles in the bloody confrontations of the Lincoln County War a century ago. Large by today's standards, the 48,000-acre spread possesses its own post office and landing strip.

Buddy Mays

Buddy Mays

Above, sailors race their colorful catamarans on peaceful Heron Lake, home of the New Mexico Sailing Club, one of two major sailing clubs in the state. Right, a sailplane glides high in the sunset. The National Soaring Foundation has its headquarters in Hobbs, the hub of Lea County in the southeast corner of the state. Hobbs is to soaring as, say, Taos is to skiing, or as Santa Fe is to art, local soarers boast. Pilots from the U.S., Europe, and Japan come here year round to take advantage of the nearly perfect soaring conditions, and gliders compete annually in a soaring contest in late June. A special 8,800-foot-long ramp at Hobbs Industrial Air Park serves as launch site for the gliders. The powerful thermal updrafts on which the sailplanes soar rise to 18,000 feet or more.

THE VAST OUTDOORS

In New Mexico we pride ourselves on being different. Where else, after all, would you find yourself actually invited to dig up and carry off part of a state park? Yet that's exactly what happens at Rock Hound State Park, near Deming in the mineral-rich Little Florida Mountains. Geodes, jasper, agate, carnelian, rhyolite, and other treasures are yours for the taking there (in modest amounts, that is; no moving vans full, please).

Rockhounding's just one of dozens of outdoor activities pursued enthusiastically throughout the state, where elevations range from a mere 2,876 feet above sea level to over 13,000 feet. Mountains and valleys, lakes and rivers, prairies and deserts all beckon devotees of the outdoors. The vast panoramas, the range from low desert to high mountain peaks, the colored, contoured rock formations, the rich detail at every turn—all this could keep a photographer happy for oh, say, a thousand years. Campers, rock climbers, botanists, biologists, hunters, fishermen, petroglyph seekers, spelunkers, hang gliders, bicyclists, runners, and a dozen other varieties of people who thrive outside flock here to enjoy our bountiful outdoors and expansive blue skies. Even those hundreds of visitors who come here each summer primarily to attend Santa Fe's famous opera find themselves sitting more-or-less outdoors in a spacious open-air opera house, where the audience often spends scene changes admiring the spectacular sunsets.

Cities, towns, and villages take up less than one-tenth of the state's space, so wildlife has plenty of room to frolic here, too. Six national wildlife refuges protect vulnerable and endangered species like the whooping cranes, which typically arrive at Bosque del Apache and Sevilleta, near Socorro, in late October and stay until mid-February. Because New Mexico encompasses so many different life zones, it supports one of the most diverse populations of mammals and other creatures in the world, biologists say. The deer and the antelope still play here, as do bighorn sheep and elk. Down in the lower desert and in the mountains of the south, javelinas (also called collared peccaries—they're something like wild boars, though not so ferocious) nibble on the fruit of the prickly pear and savor the nutritious century plant. Traveling in bands, they move easily back and forth across the international boundary between New Mexico and Mexico; for them it simply doesn't exist.

Raccoons (once known as "miners' cats" because miners kept ringtails as pets), foxes, weasels, skunks, porcupines, beavers, ermine, and muskrat all have their own bio-niche here. Badgers and coyotes, both of which eat rodents, even team up sometimes to go shopping for food. The coyote scouts out an occupied rodent burrow, the badger digs down, and the coyote grabs the prey as it tries to slip out the back door.

Mountain lions, bobcats, wild turkeys, wild horses, raptors galore . . . the list of New Mexico's animal residents would cover pages, because the state serves as habitat or partial habitat for about 140

Cliff Palmer

A historic steam engine of the Cumbres and Toltec Scenic Railroad chugs up an incline in the southern Rocky Mountains. The popular narrow-gauge railroad dates back to 1880 and is jointly owned today by the states of Colorado and New Mexico. From June through early October the C&TSRR carries travelers daily through the remote, wild high country between Chama, New Mexico, and Antonito, Colorado. In autumn the route glows with the gold of changing aspen leaves.

species of mammals and 435 species of birds, not to mention reptiles, arachnids, insects, and such. And as if we didn't have enough wildlife already, a few more species have been imported—but with good reason, hunters say. Today exotic animals like Barbary sheep (native to north Africa), Siberian and Persian ibex, and the African oryx roam remote areas of the state, providing prized trophies for hunters each year.

Hunting and fishing are both popular pastimes here, with about 153,000 hunters and 360,000 anglers heading for their favorite hunting grounds and water holes annually—though many people prefer to hunt with their cameras or sketch pads instead of guns or bows. Over 1,600 creeks, drains, lakes, streams, rivers, and reservoirs offer fishermen the chance to bag their limits of trout, catfish, pike, kokanee salmon and other game fish. Clear, cool, moonlit summer nights find many fishermen out casting their lures or bait into the dark water in hopes of nabbing a bass.

Summer nights—and days—also find backpackers and wilderness lovers out in force, particularly in the popular Pecos Wilderness area of the Santa Fe National Forest and the Gila Wilderness in the Gila National Forest. Less frequently visited, but equally alluring wildernesses include the Blue Range Wilderness of Apache and Gila National Forests near Quemado in

Richard C. Sandoval

the western part of the state and the Dome Wilderness in Santa Fe National Forest.

Camping, fishing, and hunting are permitted in most wilderness areas, but motorized vehicles of all sorts are forbidden—and you may hang glide *over* a wilderness area, but you're not allowed to land in one. Access is by foot, mule, horseback, or llama, another introduced species that thrives in New Mexico, at least at high altitudes.

Throughout the state the weather can change suddenly,

Russell Bamert

Savoring the fragrance of wildflowers and the friendly company of a cooling breeze, bicyclists experience the outdoors firsthand as they pedal around the state (left). Above, horses and riders lean into a turn at Ruidoso Downs, site each year of a busy—and dramatic—season of horseracing which includes quarterhorse racing's Triple Crown. The competition begins in mid-May and ends Labor Day with the All-American Futurity, the world's richest horse race: a $2.5 million purse. Racing seasons at the state's six tracks are sufficiently staggered so that horses cross the finish line somewhere in New Mexico year round.

A hang glider sails at sunset (above). Santa Fe, Ruidoso, Cochiti Lake, Grants, and Socorro are all popular hang-gliding centers. But Sandía Crest tops them all, aficionados say. The height of the Crest and the upward lift of New Mexico's famous thermals give enthusiasts a chance to try some of the world's best hang gliding—and to pit their own soaring skills against those of the area's resident golden eagles. On the ground (right), the state's rocks, ridges, mountains, and precipices keep rock climbers and hikers scrambling.

year round. Rangers at Chaco Culture National Historical Park, not far from the colorful Bisti Badlands in the northwest corner of the state, like to remind visitors that it's been known to freeze in the relatively low-lying region every month but July. More typical of summer throughout the state, though, are the billowing thunderheads that bring lightning, rain, and cooler air. It may be true, as wilderness lovers say, that there's no more glorious sound than the echoing of thunder reverberating through the remote canyons of the Gila—but it's not particularly glamorous for those who come unprepared.

Welcome to our vast outdoors. ⚐

Greg Sorber

Mark Mocho

Mark Nohl

Yahoo!! Summer signals rodeo time in
New Mexico. Around the state hundreds
of cowpokes compete in bronc riding,
calf roping, bull riding, steer wrestling,
barrel racing, and other popular events.
Adding a Native American touch, the
Jicarilla Apaches in the north and the
Mescalero Apaches in the south host All-
Indian Rodeos in July, followed by
August's popular rodeo in Gallup at the
Inter-Tribal Indian Ceremonial. Other
Old West events include western gunfights
in the Old Town Plaza in Albuquerque
on Sundays year round, Lincoln's
annual early August reenactment of
Billy the Kid's last jailbreak, old-time
fiddlin' contests here and there around
the state, and finger-lickin', belly-fillin'
watermelon feeds.

Steve Miller

Backpackers hop from rock to rock in the Middle Fork of the
Gila River. The Gila National Forest, through which the three
forks of the river run, includes three wilderness areas. Historic
Silver City is the major gateway to Gila country. Right, a gentle
morning mist nourishes the forest in the Aldo Leopold
Wilderness region of the Gila.

J.J. Meyers

Above, a bell tower at the two-century-old adobe Church of San Francisco de Asís in Ranchos de Taos. Adobe churches, often with pitched tin roofs, survive in many villages around the state. For centuries before the Spanish arrived, the Indians built homes of adobe and stone, and the adobe tradition remains strong today.

PRESERVATION AND GROWTH

For centuries, lifestyles in New Mexico have attracted outside attention. Spanish explorers in the 1500s marveled at the stone and adobe houses, fine cotton weavings, excellent health, longevity, and herbal medicines of the Pueblo Indians. Three centuries later, when control of the region passed from Spain to Mexico in 1821, Anglo trappers, traders, and explorers began arriving from the East along the Santa Fe Trail. Their journals and reports overflow with surprised comments about life in New Mexico.

New Mexicans were so friendly, so hospitable, the newcomers from the East wrote, so willing to suggest, "Mi casa es su casa"; my house is your house. The women considered themselves—and were considered—equals of men. These remarkable females had their own occupations and their own money, and sometimes they actually—God forbid!—smoked tobacco. Most surprising (and most suspicious), people here acted as if life was fun. Men, women, and children all seemed to be having a wickedly good time. More dances, parties, socializing, and promenading took place here in a month than went on in a year back home. The newcomers were distrustful, but intrigued.

Today, a century and a half after Anglos began adding their influence to the already centuries-old blend of Spanish and Indian cultures here, New Mexico is one of the ten fastest growing states in the nation. People from other parts of the country and world are still talking about, and being attracted by, lifestyles here. Santa Fe Style, Albuquerque Style, Old West Style, New West Style, Pueblo Style, Adobe Style, Spanish Style: all describe some dimension of life in New Mexico. According to outsiders' reports, life here is still both exotic and enticing.

All this attention makes many New Mexicans—from those whose ancestors have lived here since well before the founding of Rome to recent arrivals—understandably nervous. Life here is indeed pleasant, on the whole, and we'd like to make sure it stays that way. This concern translates itself into a desire to control economic and population growth without stifling either. To maintain the clean air, blue skies, open spaces, and unique cultural mix without denying the historical inevitability of change.

Clean industry, high tech, and novel enterprises like the development of European-style vineyards are the key to a successful balancing act, many believe. Today the Río Grande Corridor, a much-talked of dream among those who seek to develop the state economically, has become a reality, as the 500-kilometer (300-mile) stretch of the Río Grande from Los Alamos to Las Cruces becomes a center for the transfer of technology from the laboratory to the marketplace. Facilities in the Corridor include such organizations as the Terminal Effects Research and Analysis Group, the Center of Technical Excellence in High Technology Materials and Non-Invasive Medical Diagnosis, and the Center of Technical Excellence in Computer Applications and Plant Genetic Engineering. Favorable tax structures,

Mark Nohl

A traditional kiva fireplace in a new state-of-the-art photovoltaic, active solar home in Eldorado, a solar community south of Santa Fe (above and below right). The soft lines, rounded corners, brick floors, latillas (narrow ceiling boards), and vigas (large round beams) pictured here are longstanding features of adobe homes in northern New Mexico.

Mark Nohl

the high quality of life in New Mexico, and the cost-effective labor base lure investors in growing numbers from other states and abroad.

Another approach to the problem of balancing growth with preservation is the determined focus around the state on cultural enrichment and cultural conservation. Besides operas, orchestras, performing groups, festivals, and art galleries, the state abounds in museums—over a hundred in all. Even moderately sized towns like Abiquiú, Cimarrón, Capitán, Galisteo, Madrid, and Pinos Altos include museums in their repertoire of attractions. And settlements too small to maintain formal museums often serve as living museums, cultural islands in which Anglo, Hispanic, and Indian lifestyles from decades or centuries past live on.

At the heart of the state's informal network of museums are the museums of Albuquerque (including the long-awaited Natural History Museum, scheduled to open soon, the Maxwell Museum of Anthropology, and the Albuquerque Museum) and the Museum of New Mexico. Besides operating five monuments state wide (Coronado, Fort Sumner, Fort Selden, Jémez, and Lincoln), the Museum of New Mexico system includes four museums, all in Santa Fe, all dedicated to preserving special aspects of unique lifestyles: the Museum of

A classic Victorian home in Huning Highlands, a thirty-square-block section of Albuquerque listed on the National Register of Historic Landmarks. The Highlands date back to the 1880s, when Albuquerque—and other parts of New Mexico—experienced a growth spurt following the arrival of the railroad.

International Folk Art, which has gained worldwide recognition since the 1982 opening of the new Girard Wing; the Laboratory of Anthropology, soon to be augmented by the new Museum of Indian Arts and Culture; the Fine Arts Museum, home to a vast collection of Southwest art; and the historic Palace of the Governors, which dates back to 1610 and has served variously as headquarters for Spanish, Indian, Mexican, and U.S. Territorial governments. Even the Confederates controlled the Palace briefly during the Civil War.

Colorful, diverse, complicated—New Mexico brims with variety in people, backgrounds, opinions, and lifestyles, in possibilities for the future and traditions from the past. For those not yet fully acquainted with the state, a doubleheaded caveat applies as well today as it did four centuries ago, when the first Europeans here looked and listened in awe and surprise. Don't believe everything you hear about us; but don't imagine for a moment you've heard all there is to hear. ⚓

Historic La Mesilla, outside Las Cruces. Settled in the 1850s, La Mesilla was once an important stopping place for stagecoach traffic enroute to and from San Antonio, Santa Fe, and Chihuahua.

The famous Mabel Dodge Luhan house in Taos (above, left, and below), now known as Las Palomas de Taos. Once a gathering place for celebrities and literati like D.H. Lawrence and Lady Dorothy Brett, the 17-room, 8,400-square-foot adobe home today provides bed-and-breakfast accommodations for travelers to Taos. Right, ruins of the mission church at Pecos Pueblo in Pecos National Monument. Towa-speaking Indians lived in the Pueblo from about A.D. 1100 until 1838, when the twenty surviving members of the war and disease-ravaged band moved to Jémez Pueblo.

Mark Nohl

Above, White Sands National Monument. Back cover, the waxy white flowers of blossoming yucca plants, photo by Mark Nohl.

EPILOGUE

What is New Mexico? It's the evening star near the mountaintops in the west, the full moon rising in the flatlands in the east, the orange of the sunset fading out in fingered rays, the sense of a season beginning to change. It's a cloud hanging over a mesa top, roads that disappear into magical red hills, the play of the shadows on a mountainside, sunrise on the plains. Farmers, cattlemen, orchardists, scientists, engineers, businessmen, artists, writers, dreamers: speaking in many languages, coming from many cultures.

What is New Mexico? It's the sound of happy voices, solemn voices talking rapidly in Spanish about *el tiempo, los politicos, el amor, la vida, la muerte,* and above all *mis hijitos*—the weather, politicians, love, life, death, and especially mis hijitos, my children. And it's the warning in the old Spanish *dicho* (proverb). *De gota a gota se agota el mar.* Drop by drop, even the ocean goes dry.

What is New Mexico? A delicate yet durable, vulnerable yet strong land, echoing at twilight with the soft sounds of the Tewa "Song of the Loom":

> O our Mother the Earth, O our Father the Sky
> Your children are we, and with tired backs
> We bring you the gifts you love.
> Then weave for us a garment of brightness;
> May the warp be the white light of morning,
> May the weft be the red light of evening,
> May the fringes be the falling rain,
> May the border be the standing rainbow.
> Thus weave for us a garment of brightness,
> That we may walk fittingly where birds sing,
> That we may walk fittingly where grass is green,
> O our Mother the Earth, O our Father the Sky.

*For information about other **New Mexico Magazine** publications, contact **New Mexico Magazine**, Bataan Memorial Building, Santa Fe, NM 87503; (505) 827-6181. For travel and informational brochures, contact Travel Division, New Mexico Economic Development and Tourism Department, Bataan Memorial Building, Santa Fe, NM 87503; (505) 827-6230, out-of-state (800) 545-2040.*